I Feel Better

with a Frog in My Throat

History's Strangest Cures

Written and illustrated by

Carlyn Beccia

Houghton Mifflin Books for Children ❧ Houghton Mifflin Harcourt ❧ Boston New York

Instructions for use:

1. Some cures in this book are gross. Please don't eat lunch while reading.

2. Some cures in this book are painful. Please don't practice them on yourself, your pet, or family members.

3. See if you can guess which cures worked BEFORE turning the page. Don't peek. Doctors hundreds of years ago had to guess too.

4. Don't read this book while operating dangerous machinery.

5. If confusion or dizziness occurs, proceed to your nearest library for more information.

Disclaimer: Side effects from reading this book may vary. Patients may experience rapid brain growth.

Find your sickness below and turn to the correct page for a cure.

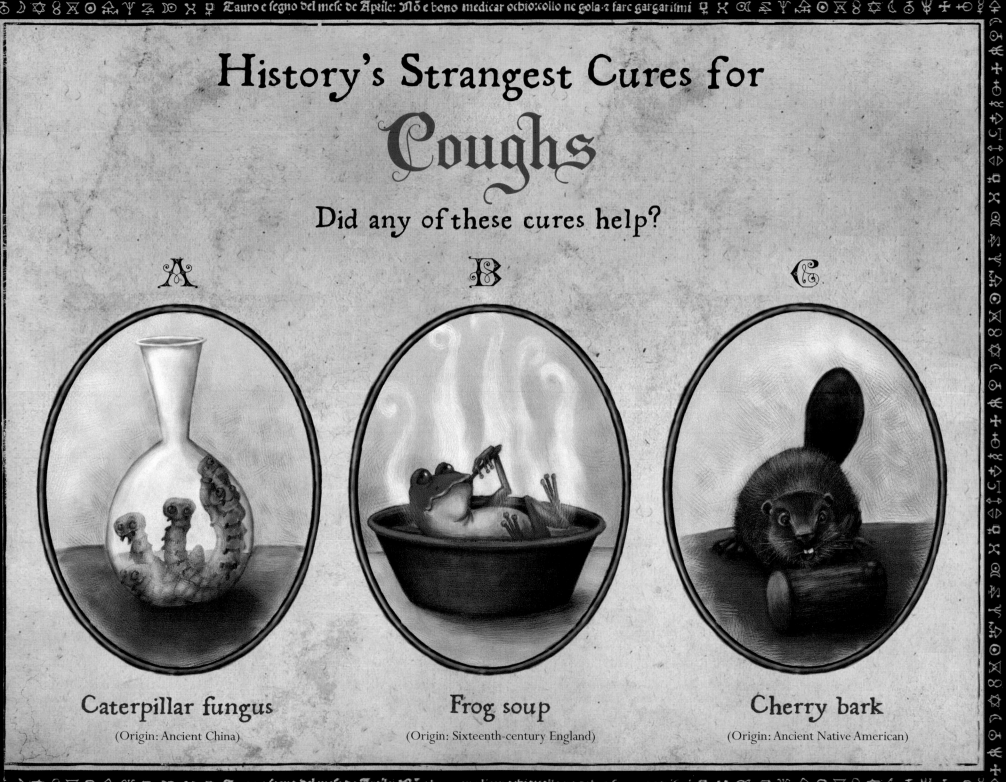

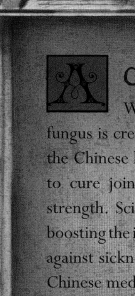

Caterpillar fungus: Maybe

When some species of caterpillar die, a fungus is created inside their bodies. For centuries, the Chinese have mixed this fungus into a medicine to cure joint pain and coughing and to increase strength. Scientists think the fungus may work by boosting the immune system — the body's protection against sickness. This cure is still used in traditional Chinese medicine today.

Frog soup: No

The medieval recipe for a cough was to make a soup out of nine frogs but not tell the diner what was in it. Although it would not have cured a cough, the extra protein would have given sick people a nutritional boost...if they could stand to swallow a frog or two.

Cherry bark: Yes

The Native Americans boiled cherry bark and drank it as a tea to treat coughs. This bark contained hydrocyanic (*high-dro-sigh-an-ic*) acid, which helps stop coughing and can be found in most modern cough and cold remedies.

History's Strangest Cures for

Colds

Did any of these cures help?

A

B

C

Chicken soup

(Origin: Medieval Europe)

Puke weed

(Origin: Sixteenth-century England)

Skunk oil

(Origin: Early-twentieth-century America)

Chicken soup: Yes

When it comes to colds, Mother is always right. While chicken soup cannot cure a cold, the broth gets rid of that awful stuffy feeling by improving the movement of nasal mucus. And when you've got the sniffles, it tastes darn good too.

Puke weed: No

Puke weed was given to sick people in the nineteenth century to do just what it sounds—make them throw up. At the time, doctors believed that colds were caused by poisons in the stomach and the best way to get rid of those poisons was to throw them up.

Skunk oil: No

In the early 1900s, people would boil a skunk and preserve the animal's fat in jars. The greasy oil was then applied to the chest. Although it is certain that it did not cure a cold, the smell would get you out of bed pretty quick.

History's Strangest Cures for
Sore Throats

Did any of these cures help?

A

B

C

A frog down
the throat

A necklace made
from earthworms

A dirty sock tied
around the neck

(Origin: Medieval Europe)

(Origin: Medieval Europe)

(Origin: Early-twentieth-century America)

A frog down the throat: Maybe

When some species of frogs get annoyed, they secrete poisonous slime out of their skin. Medieval people held a frog in a sick person's throat so that the slippery toxins could coat the throat and cure the infection. Unfortunately, the toxins mostly gave patients terrible tummy aches. Surely the frog didn't enjoy the experience either. But medieval folks were on to something. Today, frog slime is sometimes used in antibiotics and painkillers. Thankfully you can take this cure as a pill.

A necklace made from earthworms: No

In medieval Europe, the local doctor would place earthworms on a string and then tie them to the sick person's neck. Once the worms had died, the person would supposedly be cured. Most people probably forgot about the sore throat when they had worms wiggling down their shirt.

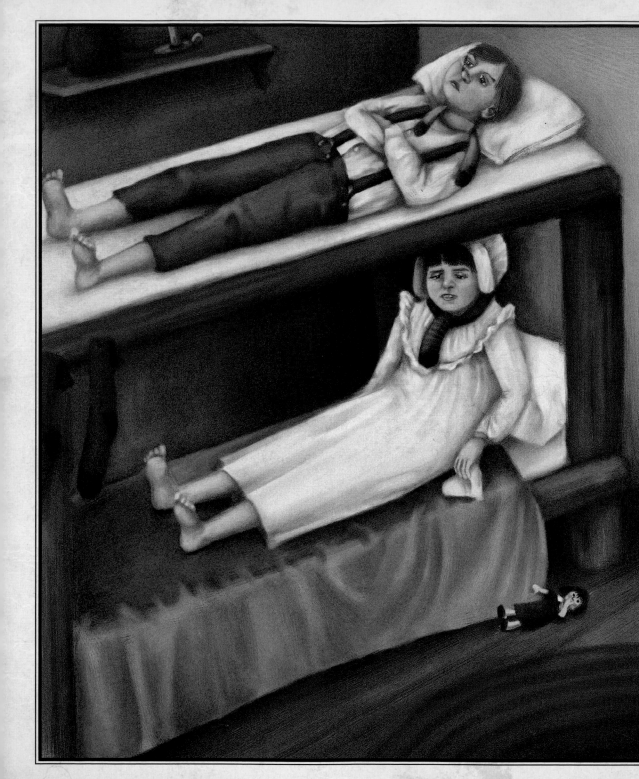

 A dirty sock tied around the neck: No

In the early 1900s, many people observed that sore throats were transferred from person to person. This observation caused people to think that a sore throat might also be transferred from a person to an animal, a plant, or in this case . . . a dirty sock. Although the smelly-sock cure did not work, it would at least make other people less likely to go near you and catch your sore throat.

The Crazy Bird Doctor

In the eighteenth century, doctors believed inhaling smelly air caused sickness. To protect against the disease-causing foul smells, doctors wore beaks filled with sweet-smelling fragrances while treating their patients. They might have looked pretty stupid dressed like a bird, but at least they were on to something . . . dirtiness led to disease.

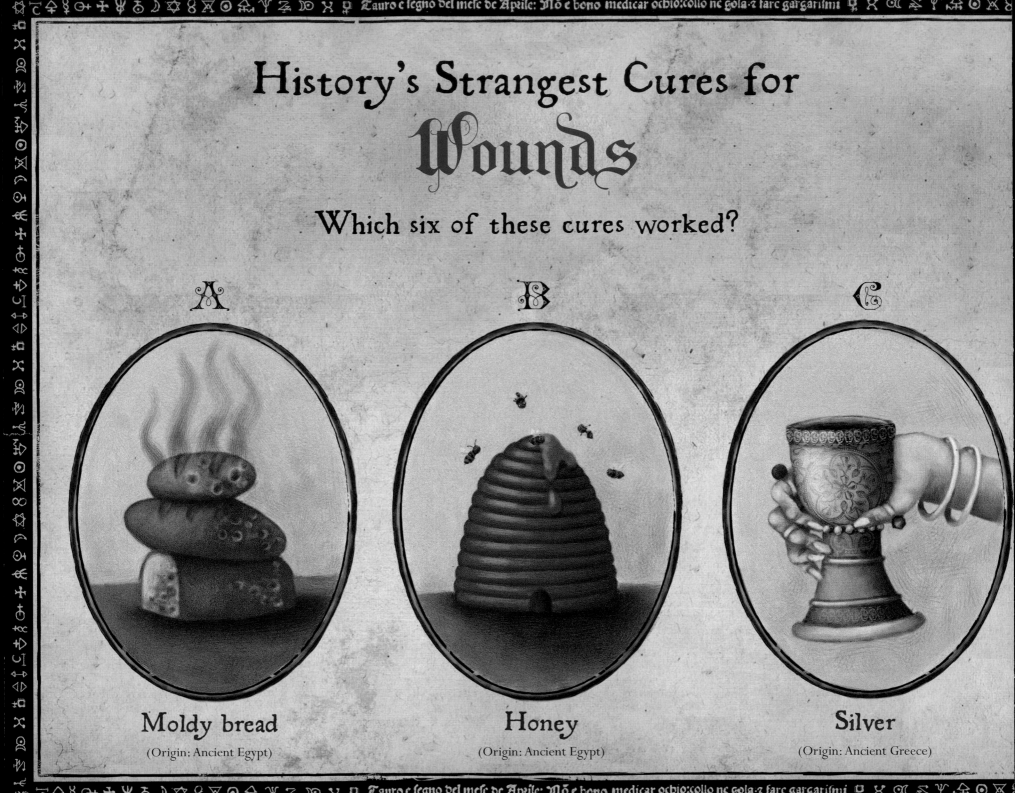

History's Strangest Cures for Wounds

Which six of these cures worked?

A

Moldy bread

(Origin: Ancient Egypt)

B

Honey

(Origin: Ancient Egypt)

C

Silver

(Origin: Ancient Greece)

D
Puppy kisses
(Origin: Ancient Greece)

E
Spider webs
(Origin: First-century Rome)

F
Mummy powder
(Origin: Early Middle Ages, Persia)

G
Maggots
(Origin: Early Middle Ages, Europe)

H
A bull's mouth
(Origin: Sixteenth-century Europe)

I
A dead man's skull
(Origin: Seventeeth-century England)

Moldy bread: Yes

Those green and black furry bits that you find on moldy bread contain small forms of an antibiotic that we call penicillin. Antibiotics, like penicillin, attack the bacteria that cause illness. The Egyptians probably did not know that penicillin existed, but they did know that putting moldy bread on deep cuts kept them from becoming infected. Doctors today have discovered several kinds of antibiotics to cure different illnesses.

Honey: Yes

The Egyptians also knew that the sugar in honey reduced swelling around a cut by soaking up fluid. It also contained small amounts of hydrogen peroxide, which killed the bad bacteria that caused infection. Scientists today are studying new ways that honey can be used in place of antibiotics.

Eye of Horus

Rx Symbol

The Eye of Horus was an ancient Egyptian symbol believed to have healing powers. Many historians believe it later evolved into the Rx symbol that we use on modern prescriptions. Do you see the similarities above?

Silver: Yes

Silver is not just a pretty metal. It also kills the bacteria that cause infection. The ancient Greeks put silver powder on wounds to help infections heal. In the Middle Ages, wealthy-born babies sucked on silver spoons to protect against plague infections. During World War I, surgeons used melted silver on wounds to keep them from becoming infected. Doctors today apply diluted silver nitrate on the skin of burn victims to speed healing and prevent infection. When you were born, doctors even put silver nitrate in your eyes to keep them from becoming infected.

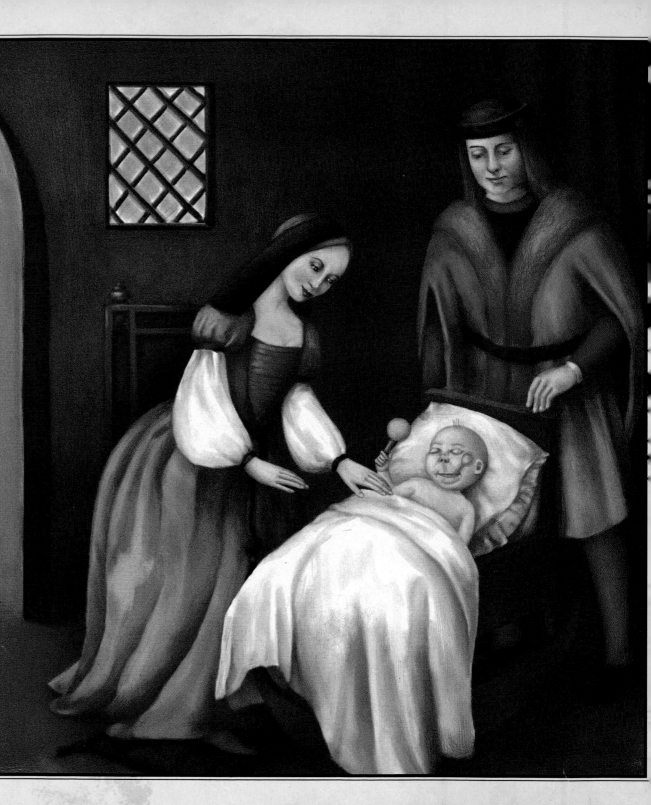

Puppy kisses: Maybe

This cure works fabulously…if you are a dog. Dogs lick their own wounds to clean them and get rid of dead tissue. Dog drool even contains germ fighters that may help heal a dog's wound, but it won't help a human's wounds heal faster and may even infect them. The ancient Greeks used this cure because they believed dogs had magical healing abilities. Wounded Greek men would rest peacefully in dark temples and wait for dogs to lick their wounds. Inscriptions left on ancient tablets even claim that this cure worked. Dog kisses probably did make the Greeks feel better. Pets comfort people, and when you are happy, you heal faster.

Spider webs: Yes

Ever walked into a spider web? Once it gets on you, it sticks like super glue. That sticky coating has been used since the first century A.D. to stop bleeding. Medieval doctors rolled the spider web into a ball and then stuffed it into the wound to stop bleeding. Scientists today believe that sometimes fungus grows on spider webs and this fungus may contain germ killers such as penicillin.

Mummy powder: No

Mummy powder did not cure wounds, and in some cases it also spread diseases. Yet even though it didn't work, doctors applied mummy powder to wounds for centuries. This cure was prescribed so often that real Egyptian mummies became scarce. To stay in business, mummy sellers were forced to grind up their grandmas or any dead person they could find.

REAL MUMM... ...ER
from Egyptian
MEDCINE

Maggots: Yes

Throughout history, a soldier's open wounds often became a delicious snack for hungry maggots. During the American Civil War, doctors observed that wounds infested with maggots healed faster. Maggots heal wounds by eating the pus and dead flesh. When dead flesh is removed, it helps new skin form over the wound.

A bull's mouth: No

In the sixteenth century, doctors believed putting an injured limb inside a bull would transfer the bull's strength to the patient and help him heal. Doctors tried this cure on King Henri III of France to treat a sore on his foot. The cure unfortunately did not work.

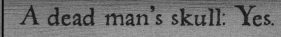

I A dead man's skull: Yes.

In seventeenth-century England, the green hairy moss that grows inside a deteriorating skull was once used to heal wounds. It is called usnea (*uhs-nee-uh*), and it helped wounds heal because it contained a bacteria-killing antibiotic that prevented infection. The Native Americans also used this cure, but they scraped the moss off trees and not skulls. You may have seen some usnea growing on trees in your own backyard.

History's Strangest Cures for Stomachaches

Did any of these cures help?

A

Urine

(Origin: Medieval Europe)

B

Dirt

(Origin: Ancient Native American)

C

Millipedes

(Origin: Seventeenth-century England)

Urine: No

Medieval doctors recommended that urine be drunk from the first pee of the morning to cure stomachaches. Although urine is sterile when it first leaves your body, this cure could make you pretty ill if you took a swig after letting it sit. Some things get better with age. Urine is not one of them. Over time, it begins to pick up bacteria that could easily make you sicker.

Dirt: Yes

Everyone knows you are not supposed to eat dirt, but people throughout history have eaten different kinds of soil and clay to cure stomachaches. The ancient Greeks ate a red clay called terra sigillata mixed with goat's blood to ease stomach pain caused from eating poison. The ancient Chinese and Native Americans ate a white clay that soothed the stomach by absorbing bacteria and also provided mineral nutrients during food shortages. You too may have eaten some dirt recently. The main ingredient in some clay, magnesium, can still be found on drugstore shelves today in products such as Philips milk of magnesia.

Monkey see...
Monkey do

How did doctors know how to cure tummy aches with dirt? They may have learned from watching animals. Elephants will often travel miles to find nutritious clays that kill toxins. Sick cattle that lack certain minerals in their diet will often lick clay. And chimpanzees eat soil to maintain their health and rid themselves of parasites.

 ## Millipedes: No

Doctors from the Middle Ages advised drinking a glass of water containing fifty live millipedes. Don't expect this cure to make your stomach feel better.

A Wormy Cure

Doctors today might not prescribe millipedes for an upset stomach, but they might someday have you drink some delicious whipworm eggs. Scientists are studying how whipworm eggs cure irritable bowel syndrome—a condition that causes terrible stomach pain. Scientists have learned that the whipworm releases a protein that soothes an upset stomach.

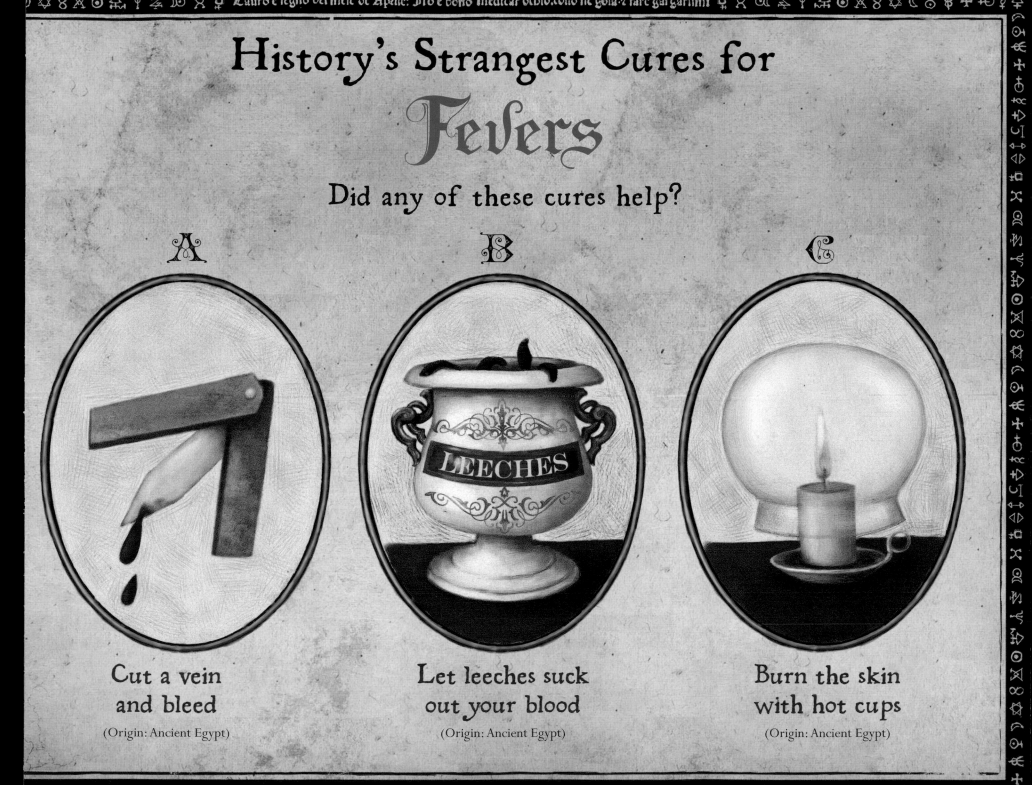

History's Strangest Cures for
Fevers

Did any of these cures help?

A

B

C

Cut a vein
and bleed

Let leeches suck
out your blood

Burn the skin
with hot cups

(Origin: Ancient Egypt)

(Origin: Ancient Egypt)

(Origin: Ancient Egypt)

Cut a vein: Sometimes

To cure a fever, doctors from ancient Egypt to the late-nineteenth century often cut a vein with a small knife called a lancet and let the blood drip out into a bowl. This cure often weakened the patient to the point of fainting, and if too much blood was taken it could even kill him. So how could a cure survive 2,500 years if it was so dangerous?

When a person is sick with an infection, a nasty bacteria called *Staphylococcus aureus* (staph) looks for lunch inside the body. Staph feeds on a specific type of iron found in blood called heme iron. If it cannot find heme iron, it starves. When doctors bled their patients, they may have temporarily starved the staph bacteria. And the patients actually felt better at first, because bloodletting lowered the body's temperature.

A very bloody cure

Today, we think of blood loss as a bad thing, but the practice of intentionally causing blood loss, called bloodletting, was once the most common cure for fevers. From around 400 B.C. to the late-seventeenth century, doctors wrongly believed that the body was made up of four different types of fluids called humours. The four humours were blood (made in the heart), phlegm (made in the head), black bile (made in the spleen), and yellow bile (made in the liver). Too much or too little of one colored fluid would cause the humours to become unbalanced and the patient to become ill. When you have a fever, your forehead will often become hot and sweaty. Doctors reasoned the extra blood was cooking the body from the inside like a pot of water boiling over. The solution was simple: get rid of the extra blood and the person would cool down. *The fever cures on the following pages were ways of getting rid of blood.*

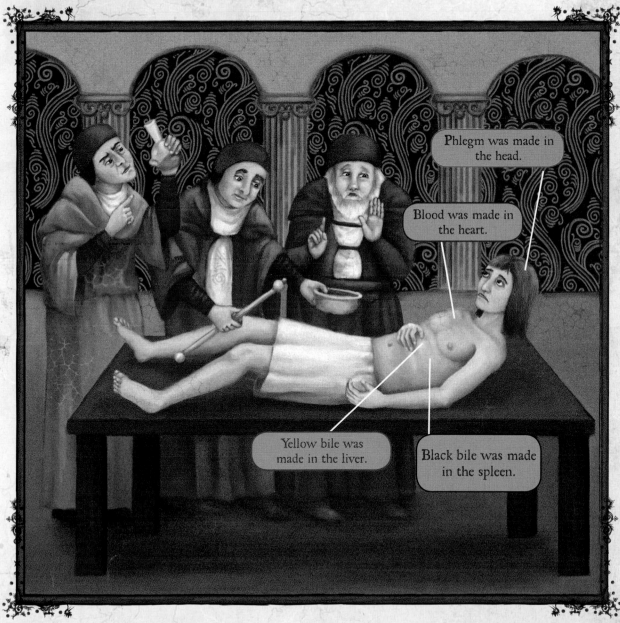

Leeches: No

Throughout history, it was believed that bloodsucking worms called leeches could suck the fever out of a person. A leech will only suck up about one ounce of blood (about a teaspoon) before they become full and fall off. This small amount is not enough to starve *Staphylococcus aureus,* so you would have to put A LOT of leeches on someone to starve a staph infection.

Four Thousand Years of Leeches

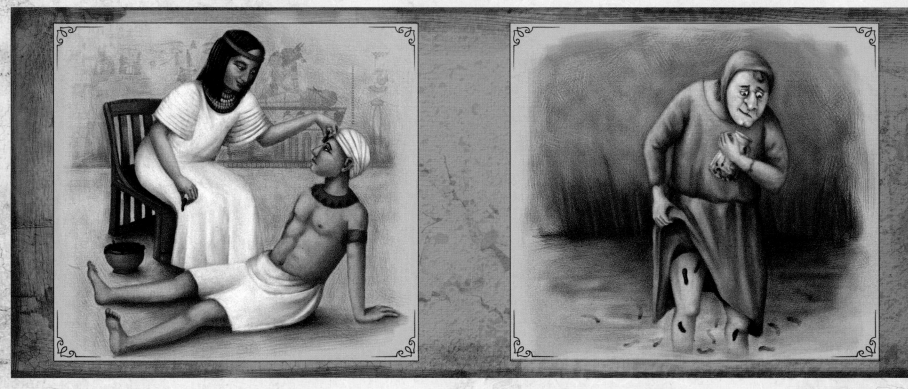

Ancient Egyptian Leeches

Four-thousand-year-old Egyptian wall paintings show leeches being applied to the patient's head and face, but archaeologists do not know if they were used as medicine or as part of a religious ceremony.

Medieval Leeches

In medieval times, a person called a leech collector would wade into leech-infested waters and wait for leeches to attach to his legs. He would then pick the leeches off, put them in a jar, and sell them.

Hungry Leech

Leeches can be as small as a quarter of an inch.

Full Leech

After a meal, they can grow up to five or six times their original size.

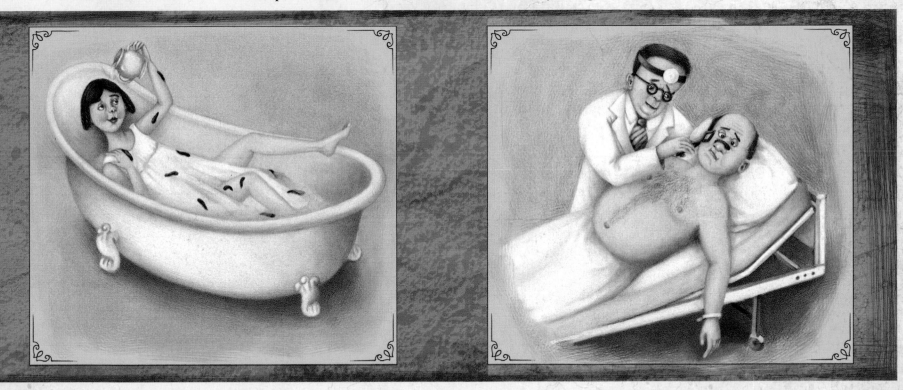

Eighteenth-Century Leeches

In the late-eighteenth century, people took leech baths full of bloodsuckers just to stay healthy. By the nineteenth century, leeches became so popular that doctors almost ran out of them.

Modern Leeches

Doctors today might prescribe leeches to help repair damaged tissue on an ear or nose. When a leech sucks on injured flesh, it releases special proteins into its saliva that prevent dangerous blood clots from forming.

Cupping: No

In medieval times, glass cups were heated under a flame and then applied to the skin in a process called cupping. Doctors believed that the cups drew the sickness out of the body because the heat forced the blood to the surface of the skin. In reality, cupping only left painful red welts on the poor victim's skin.

History's Strangest Cures for
Headaches

Did any of these cures help?

A

B

C

A hole in the
head

Mustard on the
head

A shock from an
electric eel

(Origin: Prehistoric man)

(Origin: Ancient Greece)

(Origin: Ancient Rome)

A hole in the head: No

Prehistoric man believed headaches were caused by little demons trapped inside the head. Their solution was simple: make a hole in the head so the demons could escape. All it took was a few good whacks on the noggin with a sharp stone. Unfortunately, a hole in the head didn't cure a headache, and if the patient was really unlucky, it could kill him.

Fig. 1

By the eighteenth century, the process of drilling a hole in the head was called trepanning, but doctors used hand cranks instead of a sharp rock. In rare cases, doctors today may make a hole in a patient's head to relieve pressure on the brain. The operation is done with an electric drill, and unlike with past procedures, the removed bone is always put back in place.

Mustard on the head: No

Mustard has been applied to skin throughout history to cure headaches. Mustard was mixed with water, flour, or eggs to make a goopy paste called a mustard plaster. The plaster was brushed on one side of a cloth, and then the other side was applied to the skin. Mustard plasters drew the blood to the surface of the skin and gave the patient a nice warming sensation. But apply too much and the heat caused painful blisters. Doctors of the nineteenth and twentieth centuries believed that these blisters drew the illness out of the head. They thought if it hurt, then it must be working.

I was suffering very severely with a sick headache, and stopped at a farm house on the road some distance to the rear of the main body of the army. I spent the night in bathing my feet in hot water and mustard, and putting mustard plasters on my wrists and the back part of my neck, hoping to be cured by morning.

—Ulysses S. Grant

Presidential Mustard Plaster

Our eighteenth president and Civil War general, Ulysses S. Grant, was one tough cookie. He ate cucumbers soaked in vinegar for breakfast, drove his horse at breakneck speeds, and was not afraid of using painful mustard plasters to cure his raging headaches. The above excerpt is an entry from his wartime journal.

A shock from an electric eel: Maybe

Ancient Romans believed that a zap from a species of electric eel called a black torpedo fish would numb headache pain. Sound shocking? Maybe. But doctors today are researching ways in which small electrical currents could ease pain in headache suffers.

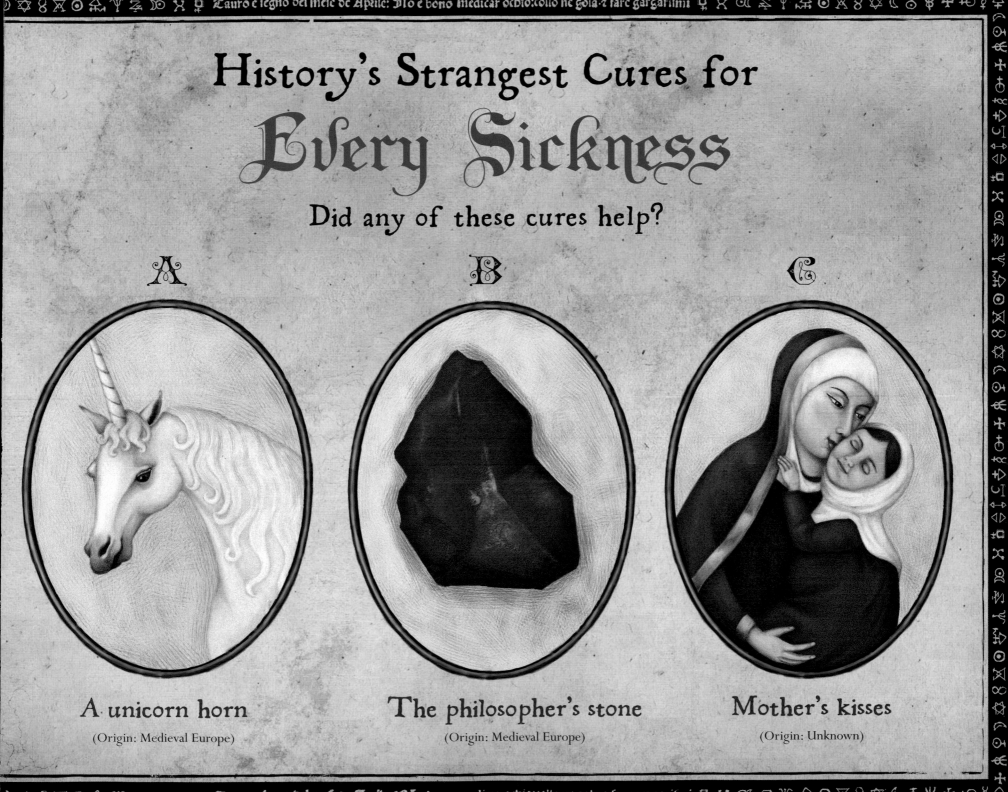

History's Strangest Cures for
Every Sickness

Did any of these cures help?

A

B

C

A unicorn horn

(Origin: Medieval Europe)

The philosopher's stone

(Origin: Medieval Europe)

Mother's kisses

(Origin: Unknown)

 A unicorn horn: No

Noblemen drank from a unicorn horn, believing that the horn would sweat if their drink was poisoned. Sometimes they ground up the tip of the horn and drank it to make them strong and heal any sickness. Unicorn horns were extremely rare because they could only be captured by a beautiful maiden. Luckily a rhino or narwhal could be captured by any ugly old slob, because it was really their tusks being sold.

A rhinoceros horn was prized as medicine and often sold as a "unicorn horn."

A narwhal is a species of arctic whale with a long tusk that can grow to up to ten feet long.

The philosopher's stone: No

Men who mixed chemicals, called alchemists, believed that a secret stone called the philosopher's stone could turn metal into gold and even make people live forever. Believing the stone was hidden in urine, they collected barrels of urine from local soldiers and heated them in hopes of finding gold. Unfortunately, the philosopher's stone was never found.

Mother's kisses through history: Yes

Scientific studies show that kisses can help people heal faster. Scientists even have a name for this mysterious phenomenon—the placebo effect. The placebo effect works by making you believe the cure is working. When your brain believes, it sends signals to the rest of your body to hurry up and heal, and your body really listens. So next time you know someone who is not feeling well, don't go hunting for some maggots. Give the person a kiss. It just might be the one medicine that will make her feel better.

Prehistoric kisses   Ancient kisses   Medieval kisses

"He is the best physician who is the most ingenious inspirer of hope."
—Samuel Taylor Coleridge

Renaissance kisses   Nineteenth-century kisses   Today's kisses

To Charlotte and John — who always make me feel better. And to my husband, John, who patiently listened to all my wacky medical advice.

Houghton Mifflin Books for Children is an imprint of Houghton Mifflin Harcourt Publishing Company.

www.hmhbooks.com

The text of this book is set in Perpetua.
The illustrations are digital mixed media.
Library of Congress Cataloging-in-Publication Data is on file.
ISBN 978-0-547-22570-8
Manufactured in China
LEO 10 9 8 7 6 5 4 3
4500341405

The history of medicine is not a simple tale with a beginning and an end. From the moment the first cavemen stood upright, it has continued to evolve and will do so as long as man seeks progress. As trade routes opened up with China and India, Western medicine borrowed many of its practices from traditions steeped in ancient remedies. I have chosen to focus this story primarily on Western medicine because it succeeded in spreading and recording its practices with the invention of the printing press. I have done my best to track the origins of all cures, but origins are difficult to pinpoint without written records. I encourage readers to explore some of the further reading about medicine listed on my website www.Ifeelbetterbook.com.

Select Bibliography

Ackerknecht, Erwin H., M.D. *A Short History of Medicine.* Baltimore: Johns Hopkins University Press, 1955.

Anderson, John Q. "Magical Transference of Disease in Texas Folk Medicine." *Western Folklore* 27, no. 3 (1968): 191–99.

Dharmananda, Subhuti, Ph.D. "Safety Issues Affecting Herbs. Usnea: An Herb Used in Western and Chinese Medicine." Institute for Traditional Medicine, Portland, Oregon. Accessed online at www.itmonline.org/arts/usnea.htm.

Glembocki, Vicki L. "Arachnicillin." *Research/Penn State* 16, no. 3 (1995). Accessed online at www.rps.psu.edu/sep95/arachnicillin.html.

Gunther, Theodore Robert, and John Goodyer. *The Greek Herbal of Dioscorides.* New York: Hafner Publishing, 1959.

Inglis, Brian. *A History of Medicine.* Cleveland: World Publishing Company, 1965.

Jackson, William. "The Use of Unicorn Horn in Medicine." *Pharmaceutical Journal* 273 (2004): 18–25.

Janos, Elisabeth. *Country Folk Medicine: Tales of Skunk Oil, Sassafras Tea, and Other Old-Time Remedies.* Gilford, Conn.: Lyons Press, 1990.

Jianzhe Ying and Xiaolan Mao. *Icons of Medical Fungi from China.* Beijing: Science Press, 1987.

Lieberman, Janet J., and Stanley J. Lieberman. "A Short History of Quackery and Byways in Medicine." *American Biology Teacher* 37, no. 1 (1975): 39–43.

Magner, Louis. *A History of Medicine.* Boca Raton, Fla.: Taylor & Francis, 2005.

Pollington, Stephen. *Leechcraft: Early English Charms, Plant-lore and Healing.* Norfolk, U.K.: Anglo-Saxon Books, 2000.

Porter, Roy. *Blood and Guts: A Short History of Medicine.* New York: W. W. Norton, 2002.

Root-Bernstein, Robert and Michele. *Honey, Mud, Maggots, and Other Medical Marvels: The Science Behind Folk Remedies and Old Wives' Tales.* Boston: Houghton Mifflin, 1997.

Seigworth, Gilbert R., M.D. "Bloodletting over the Centuries." *New York State Journal of Medicine* 13 (1980): 2022–28. Accessed online at www.pbs.org/wnet/redgold/basics/bloodlettinghistory.html.

Steele, Volney, M.D. *Bleed, Blister, and Purge.* Missoula, Mont.: Mountain Press Publishing, 2005.

Thorwald, Jurgen. *Science and Secrets of Early Medicine.* New York: Harcourt, Brace & World, 1962.

Turner, E. S. *The Astonishing History of the Medical Profession.* New York: Ballantine Books, 1961.

Schaffer, Amanda. "It May Come as a Shock." *New York Times,* November 7, 2006. Accessed online at www.nytimes.com/2006/11/07/health/07migr.html.

Van der Geer, Alexandra, and Michael Dermitzakis. "Fossil Medicines from 'Snake Eggs' to 'Saint's Bones': An Overview." *Calicut Medical Journal* 6, no. 1 (2008): e8.

Wadd, William. *Mems. Maxims, and Memoirs.* London: Oxford University, 1827.

West, Susan. "How Are Kings and Marine Algae Alike?" *Science News* 115, no. 12 (1979): 189.

Wilbur, C. Keith, M.D. *Revolutionary Medicine 1700–1800.* Chester, Conn.: Globe Pequot Press, 1980.